To/

HAPPY
BIRTHDAY

Take a trip back in time to the year you were born, 1941.

Happy 80th Birthday - enjoy reminiscing.

Lots of love,

80 YEARS AGO BACK IN 1941

WORLD MAP

World Population

2.3 BILLION

Britain population

48.2 MILLION

2021

World Population

7.8 BILLION

Britain population

67.61 MILLION

MAJOR WORLD LEADERS

UK- PM WINSTON CHURCHHILL

US- PRESIDENT FRANKLIN D. ROOSEVELT

RUSSIA/SOVIET UNION - JOSEPH STALIN

ITALY - PM BENITO MUSSOLINI

GERMANY - ADOLF HITLER

CANADA -PM WILLIAM LYON MCKENZIE KING

SOUTH AFRICA - PM FIELD MARSHALL JAN CHRISTIAAN SMUTS

MEXICO - MANUEL AVILA CAMACHO

JAPAN - FUMIMARO KONOE / HIDEKI TOLO

You Have Been Loved for

80 YEARS

Thats 960 months

4174 Weeks | **29,220** days

701,280 hrs

42,076,800 MINUTES

2,524,608,000 SECONDS

and counting...

80 & Fabulous

Dame Vivienne Westwood

Born in 1941

British Fashion Designer

Largely responsible for bringing modern punk fashion into the mainstream.

Charles Robert Watts

Born in London 2nd June 1941

Musician/Drummer

Best known as member of The Rolling Stones

Sir Alex Ferguson

Born in Glasgow on 31st December 1941

Footballer and Manager

Widely known for managing Manchester United from 1986 to 2013

He is considered by many to be one of the greatest managers of all time.

Miriam Margolyes OBE

Born in Oxford 18th May 1941

Actress and Comedian

May roles acrossTheatre, Film and Television

David Dickinson

Born in Stockport August 16th 1941

Antiques Expert and

Television Presenter

Known for shows such as Bargain Hunt & Dickinson's Real Deal.

Julia Kathleen McKenzie. CBE

Born in Middlesex on 17th February 1941

Actress, Singer and Presenter

Stared in stage shows Guys and Dolls, Sweeney Todd and TV shows French Fields and Miss Marple.

Oscars

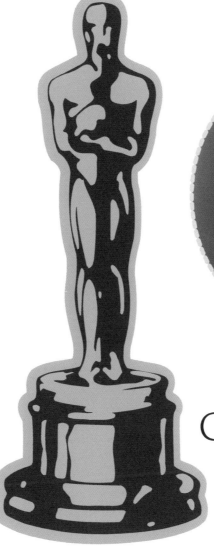

Best Actor

James Stewart

Philadelphia Story

Box Office

$3,300,00

Best Actress

Ginger Rogers

Kitty Foyle

Box Office

$2,385,000

The Thief of Bagdad

Best visual effects

Best cinematography

Best production Design

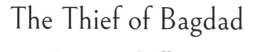

Best Original Score

Pinnochio

$164,000,000

Films

Dumbo

Initially Walt Disney was uninterested in making this movie. To get him interested, story men Joe Grant and Dick Huemer wrote up the film as instalments which they left on Walt's desk every morning. Finally, he ran in to the department saying "This is great, what happens next?"

Citizen Kane

Despite all the publicity, the film was a box-office flop and was quickly consigned to the RKO vaults. At 1941's Academy Awards the film was booed every time one of its nine nominations was announced. It was only re-released to the public in the mid-'50s.

The Maltese Falcon

Three of the statuettes still exist and are conservatively valued at over $1 million each. This makes them some of the most valuable film props ever made; indeed, each is now worth more than three times what the film cost to make.

Films 1941

Cinemas during the War

When the war was first announced in 1939 cinemas were immediately closed. Within weeks the government realised people needed entertainment and they were reopened. Cinemas enjoyed a huge boom in attendance from 1941 onwards.

In 1941 cinema admissions rose to just over 1 billion and continued to rise through the war peaking at 1.5 billion in 1943, 1944 & 1945. Cinema going was the nations prime leisure activity and it proved to be an indispensable means to instructing and informing the nation during war years.

- **Citizen Kane** starring Orson Welles, Joseph Cotten, Dorothy Comingore

- **The Lady Eve** starring Barbara Stanwyck, Henry Fonda, Charles Coburn

- **Honky Tonk** starring Clark Gable, Lana Turner, Frank Morgan

- **The Maltese Falcon** starring Humphrey Bogart, Mary Astor, Gladys George

- **Suspicion** starring Cary Grant, Joan Fontaine, Cedric Hardwicke

- **Dr. Jekyll and Mr. Hyde** starring Spencer Tracy, Ingrid Bergman, Lana Turner

- **Hold Back the Dawn** starring Charles Boyer, Olivia de Havilland, P.Goddard

- **Dumbo** Sterling Holloway, Edward Brophy, Herman Bing, Mel Blanc

- **Tobacco Road** starring Charley Grapewin, Gene Tierney, Marjorie Rambeau

- **How Green was my Valley** starring Walter Pidgeon, Maureen O'Hara, Anna Lee, Donald Crisp

Average cost of living 1941

Average House £550 - In todays money thats £27,947

Average Salary £195 - In todays money thats £9,908

Average Car price £310 - In todays money thats £15,752

Average food shop £0.39 - In todays money thats £19.82

FOOD SHOPPING

FLOUR 1.5KG £0.03 - £1.52 today

BREAD 1 LOAF £0.01 - 51p today

SUGAR 1KG £0.04 - £2.03 today

MILK 1PT £0.07 - £3.56 today

BUTTER 250G £0.04 - £2.03 today

CHEESE 400G £0.05 - £2.54 today

POTATOES 2.5KG £0.03 - £1.52 today

BACON 400G £0.12 - £6.10 today

- Total casualties for World War II are estimated between 70-80 million people, 80% of whom came from 4 countries – Russia, China, Germany & Poland. 50-55 million of the casualties were civilians, with the majority of those being women and children.

- Had it been necessary for a third atom bomb, the city targeted would have been Tokyo.

- Adolph Hitler's nephew, William Hitler served in the US Navy during World War II.

- To avoid using the German sounding name Hamburger during World War II, Americans used the name 'Liberty Steak'.

- In World War II British soldiers got a ration of 3 sheets of toilet paper per day. Americans got 22.

- Silly putty was accidentally discovered when a general Electric Engineer was trying to create synthetic rubber.

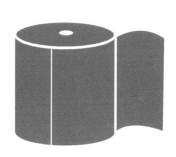

Music

Harry Lillis "Bing" Crosby Jr.

American Singer, Comedian and Actor. The first multimedia star.

Born 3rd May 1903 in Washington USA.

Biggest hit was his recording of Irving Berlin's White Christmas, first broadcast on Christmas day 1941, going on to sell over 50 million copies.

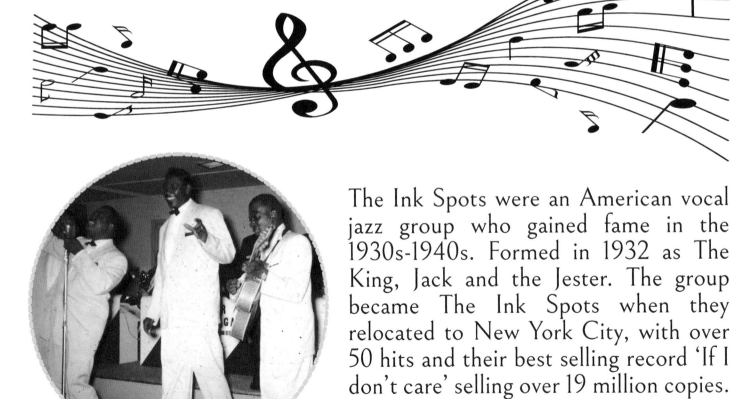

The Ink Spots were an American vocal jazz group who gained fame in the 1930s-1940s. Formed in 1932 as The King, Jack and the Jester. The group became The Ink Spots when they relocated to New York City, with over 50 hits and their best selling record 'If I don't care' selling over 19 million copies.

No 1's

Just 11 songs from only 5 artists held the top spot of No1 throughout 1941.

What was the number 1 single when you were born?
Check the list below to find out.

6th Jan-12th Jan	Bless You	Ink Spots
13th Jan-9th Feb	Whispering Grass	Ink Spots
10th Feb-23rd Feb	Pennsylvania 6-5000	Andrews Sisters
24th Feb-16th Mar	Only Forever	Bing Crosby
17th Mar-13th Apr	I'll never smile again	Ink Spots
14th Apr-25th May	We Three	Ink Spots
26th May-20th July	Waltzing In the Clouds	Deanna Durbin
21st Jul-24th Aug	It's foolish but it's fun	Deanna Durbin
25th Aug-12th Oct	Do I worry	Ink Spots
13th Oct-14th Dec	Dolores	Bing Crosby
15th Dec-22nd Dec	Yours	Vera Lynn

Fashion

While you were just a baby and dressed in nappies and babygrows. The rest of the country saw clothes rationing come in to place on the 1st June 1941. Around a quarter of men and women were entitled to wear a uniform as part of the armed forces. The style of the 40s was very much influenced by the war. The infamous make do and mend campaign was launched a couple of years later when you were just 2 (1943). Handmade and hand repaired clothing became an essential part of wartime life.

War Didn't mean the end of Fashion

The war disrupted and dislocated fashion in Britain however despite this fashion survived, flourished even with increased creativity and individual flair.

Fashion

By Autumn 1941 it became compulsory for all utility clothes to be marked 'CC41'. The logo was designed by Reginald Shipp.

When introduced the coupon allowance per person was 66 points to last one year. 11 coupons were needed for a dress, 2 for a pair of stockings, 8 for a mans shirt or pair of trousers, 5 for women's shoes while mens footwear required 7 points. This allocation shrank every year until the end of the war in 1945.

Extra coupons were given to children in recognition that they grew out of their clothes quickly, although mothers were encouraged to bigger bigger and alter to fit.

1940s mens clothing restrictions meant that jackets could not have pleated backs, metal zippers or buttons, feature raglan sleeves, or have half belts. Most men kept their clothing from the 1930s and wore them through the early '40s. It was a sign of support for the war to be seen in your pre-war suits.

Sports

1940-41 Football

By the beginning of the 1940-41 season the Battle of Britain was raging in the air and the Blitz was causing major damage throughout Britain. Coventry and Sheffield were targeted towards the end of 1940. Highfield Road was so badly damaged that Coventry city had to withdraw from the league. Sheffield United had to play at Hillborough after Bramall Lane was put out of action. This wasn't the only enforced groundshare. Highbury was turned into an Air Raid Precaution stronghold, which meant Arsenal had to play at White Hart Lane. Manchester United also had to move in with their neighbours. Old Trafford was damaged extensively in March 1941 and didn't host a football game for another 8 years.

Despite their big fan bases neither United or City could keep up with Preston in the 1940-41 season. Preston won the league and went on to complete a double by beating Arsenal in the War Cup Final.

1940-41 Scottish Football

Southern League champions - Rangers

Summer Cup Winners - Hibernian

Southern League Cup winners - Rangers

Women's Boat Race 1941

The 8th women's boat race took place on the 8th March 1941. The contest was between Oxford and Cambridge and held on the River Thames. Oxford won with a margin of 6 seconds.

1941-1942 Northern Rugby Football League.

Wartime Emergency League season.

Champions - Dewsbury

Runner up - Bradford Northern

War Time Rations

Food rationing was in place throughout 1941. On January 8th 1940 it began with bacon, ham, sugar and butter. Later in 1940 meat, tea, margarine, cooking fats and cheese were rationed. In 1941 jam, marmalade, treacle and syrup were added to the list. Then in June 1941 the distribution of eggs was controlled. In August 1941 manual workers were given an extra cheese allowance. In December 1941 national dried milk and a vitamin welfare scheme was introduced.

Despite the war ending in 1945 (when you were just 4) food rationing was still in place until 4th July 1954 which totals 14 years of food rations.

As a child you'll likely remember the joy when sweet rationing ended in 1953 (an attempt had been made to end sweet rationing in 1949 but lasted for only months as demand far outweighed supply!)

WW2 Rations 1941: per one person (adult)
Butter: 50g (2oz)
Bacon or ham: 100g (4oz)
Margarine: 100g (4oz)
Cooking fat/lard: 100g (4oz)
Sugar: 225g (8oz).
Meat: To the value of 1/2d and sometimes 1/10d – about 1lb (450g) to 12ozs (350g)
Milk: 3 pints (1800ml) occasionally dropping to 2 pints (1200ml).
Cheese: 2oz (50g) rising to 8oz (225g)
Eggs: 1 fresh egg a week.
Tea: 50g (2oz).
Jam: 450g (1lb) every two months.
Dried eggs: 1 packet (12 eggs) every four weeks.
Sweets & Chocolate: 350g (12oz) every four weeks

British Restaurants

Originally called community feeding centres, renamed by Winston Churchill; they were set up by the Ministry of Food and run by volunteers on a not-for-profit basis. Meals were sold for a max of 9d or less. By mid 1941, over 200 hundred operated in London county council area. No-one could be served with a meal of more than one serving of meat, game, poultry, fish, eggs or cheese.

Welcome to the world -1941

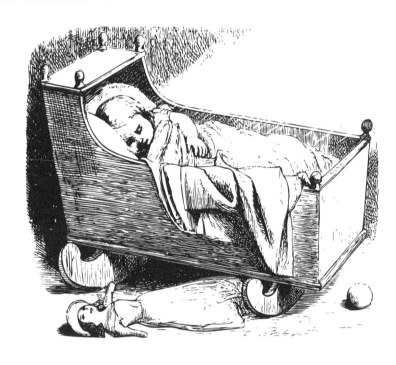

Mary
Barbara
Patricia
Carol
Linda
Judith
Betty
Nancy
Sandra
Shirley

James
Robert
John
William
Richard
Charles
David
Thomas
Ronald
Donald

War babies (1939-1945)

1941 saw the lowest birth rate at just under 700,000 births.

A normal year is approx 1 million births.

Books published 1941

The Keys of the Kingdom by A.J.Cronin (held 16 weeks at top of New York Times Fiction best sellers list)

The Sun is my Undoing by Marguerite Steen

For Whom the Bell Tolls by Ernest Hemingway

Make way for the Ducklings by Robert McCloskey

Little Town on the Prairie by Laura Ingalls Wilder

The black Stallion by Walter Farley

Evil Under the Sun by Agatha Christie

My Friend Flicka by Mary O'Hara

Escape from Freedom by Erich Fromm

Between the Acts by Virginia Woolf

Paddle-to-the-Sea by Holling Clancy Holling

Mildred Pierce by James M,Cain

Best-selling children's books included Curious George by H.A and Margaret Ray and the Crab with the Golden Claws (Tin Tin) by Herge

Toys

The 1940s began with Britain plunged into the Second World War with Germany. The war period was one of great austerity, with shortages of every kind. The toy industry was subject to the same restrictions as other industries and rationing continued long after the war ended. Most children played with toys which had been handed down from older children or made at home.

Where possible, some firms, such as Nicol Toys, were able to continue production throughout the war as long as they were permitted access to materials. Plimpton Engineering, the manufacturers of the construction set Bayko, used aluminium or tinplate instead of steel for the rods in the kits, less consistent colour and very crude packaging. By the end of 1941 however the works had gone over entirely to the war effort, producing goods including parts for Wellington bombers.

Children in the major cities soon began to be subjected to almost nightly bombing and they needed toys and games both as a distraction and morale booster. Consequently, Sir William Stephenson, chairman of Woolworths and also head of Aircraft Production for Churchill's government was instructed to find a source for materials to increase toy production. He went to his boss, Lord Beaverbrook, then publisher of the Daily Express, and asked for his help in supplying paper pulp that could be turned into toys and games. Beaverbrook agreed but only on condition that Woolworths held the price of their toys

Toys

at sixpence (2½p) for the duration of the war. Stephenson accepted those terms, and Woolworths were able to produce and sell sets that included: a cardboard boxing game which pitted a super-strong Winston Churchill against a rather feeble Adolf Hitler, a selection of Lumar patriotic jigsaw puzzles and a number of popular card games. These cheap cardboard and paper toys became increasingly important as the war progressed because, from 1942, the toy industry was not allowed to use metal.

Monopoly, had quite an interesting wartime history. Patented by Charles Darrow in 1935 as the well-known property trading game, in 1941, the British Secret Intelligence Service had John Waddington Ltd, the licensed manufacturer of the game in Britain, create a special edition for POW camps. Maps, compasses, real German money and other objects useful for escaping prisoners were hidden inside these games, which were distributed to Allied POWs by fake charity groups created and run by the British secret service.

World Events 1941

Operation Barbarossa

HITLER BEGINS OPERATION BARBAROSSA - THE INVASION OF RUSSIA. THE BLITZ CONTINUES AGAINST BRITAINS MAJOR CITIES, ALLIES TOOK TOBRUK IN NORTH AFRICA, AND RESIST GERMAN ATTACKS. JAPAN ATTACKS PEARL HARBOUR AND THE US ENTERS THE WAR.

Franklin D Roosevelt

JANUARY 22, FRANKLIN D. ROOSEVELT IS SWORN IN FOR A THIRD TERM AS PRESIDENT OF THE UNITED STATES

The Anastoff-Berry

THE ANASTOFF-BERRY COMPUTER - THE FIRST AUTOMATIC ELECTRIC DIGITAL COMPUTER WAS PROPOSED IN WRITING BY JOHN VINCENT ANASTOFF AND CLIFFORD BERRY (IT WAS IN PRODUCTION A YEAR LATER).

First penicillin patient

RESERVE CONSTABLE ALBERT ALEXANDER, A PATIENT IN THE RADCLIFFE INFIRMARY IN OXFORD BECOMES THE FIRST PERSON TO BE TREATED WITH PENICILLIN.

Elmer Pet Rabbit

THE SHORT SUBJECT ELMERS PET RABBIT IS RELEASED MARKING THE SECOND APPEARANCE OF BUGS BUNNY. WARNER BROS. MERRIE MELODIES CARTOON DIRECTED BY CHICK JONES.

Victor de Laveleye

IN A BBC RADIO BROADCAST FROM LONDON, VICTOR DE LAVELEYE ASKS BELGIANS TO USE THE LETTER V AS A RALLYING SIGN, BEING THE FIRST LETTER OF VICTORIA (VICTORY) IN FRENCH AND VRIJHEID (FREEDOM) IN DUTCH. THIS IS THE BEGINNING OF THE V CAMPAIGN WHICH SEES V GRAFFITIED ON THE WALLS OF BELGIUM . LATER ALL OF EUROPE ADOPT THE V SIGN FOR VICTORY AND FREEDOM. WINSTON CHURCHILL ADOPTS THE SIGN SOON AFTERWARDS, THOUGH SOMETIMES GETS IT THE WRONG WAY AROUND AND USES THE COMMON INSULT GESTURE!

Winston Churchill

WINSTON CHURCHILL IN A WORLDWIDE BROADCAST TELLS THE US TO SHOW ITS SUPPORT BY SENDING THE ARMS TO THE BRITISH "GIVE US THE TOOLS AND WE WILL FINISH THE JOB"

World events - Feb-May

3 night blitz - Swansea

3 NIGHT BLITZ OVER SWANSEA, SOUTH WALES. OVER THESE 3 NIGHTS OF INTENSIVE BOMBING WHICH LASTED A TOTAL OF 13 HOURS AND 48 MINUTES, SWANSEAS TOWN CENTRE IS ALMOST COMPLETELY OBLITERATED BY 869 HIGH EXPLOSIVE BOMBS.

MAR

Bill Tulle deciphers code

A GERMAN LORENZ CIPHER MACHINE OPERATOR SENDS A 4000 MESSAGE TWICE, ALLOWING BRITISH MATHEMATICIAN BILL TULLE TO DECIPHER THE MACHINES CODING MECHANISM.

MAY

Cheerios

THE BREAKFAST CEREAL CHEERIOS IS INTRODUCED AS CHEERIOATS

Rudolph Hess

RUDOLF HESS PARACHUTES INTO SCOTLAND CLAIMING TO BE ON A PEACE MISSION.

Orson Wells film

ORSON WELLS FILM CITIZEN CANE PREMIERES IN NEW YORK.

Gloster jet flight

THE FIRST BRITISH JET AIRCRAFT THE GLOSTER E.28/39 IS FLOWN.

World events - May-Aug

Bismark

German Battleship the Bismarck is sunk in the North Atlantic (it was eventually found in 1989).

HMS Hood

On May 15th In the North Atlantic, German Battleship Bismarck sinks battlecruiser HMS Hood killing all but 3 crewmen from a total of 1,418 aboard the pride of the Royal Navy

Disney Strike

The Disney Animators go on strike due to Walt Disneys refusal to recognise low pay of animators

July

Tom & Jerry

The Tom and Jerry cartoon short The midnight Snack is released; it is the second appearance for the duo in which they are officially named.

Commercial TV

NBC television begins the first commercial television.

Holocaust

The holocaust atrocities Began in 1941 through to 1945. the world wide genocide of European Jews, During this time Nazi Germany and its collaborators systematically murdered six million Jewish people.

F.Rossevelt & W.Churchill

Franklin Roosevelt snd Winston Churchill meet on board the naval station Argentinia, Newfoundland. The Atlantic charter is released setting goals for postwar international cooperation.

World events - Sep-Dec

Pentagon

CONSTRUCTION OF THE PENTAGON BEGINS IN WASHINGTON DC

Dumbo

DISNEY FILM DUMBO IS RELEASED

Winston Churchill

WINSTON CHURCHILL DECLARES "SHOULD THE US BECOME INVOLVED IN A WAR WITH JAPAN, THE BRITISH DECLARATION WILL FOLLOW WITHIN THE HOUR"

Holocaust

THE HOLOCAUST - THE REQUIREMENT TO WEAR THE STAR OF DAVID WITH THE WORD JEW INSCRIBED, IS EXTENDED TO ALL JEWS OVER THE AGE OF 6 IN GERMAN OCCUPIED AREAS.

Film - Maltese Falcon

THE HOLOCAUST - THE REQUIREMENT TO WEAR THE STAR OF DAVID WITH THE WORD JEW INSCRIBED, IS EXTENDED TO ALL JEWS OVER THE AGE OF 6 IN GERMAN OCCUPIED AREAS.

Mount Rushmore

THE LAST DAY OF CARVING ON MOUNT RUSHMORE IN SOUTH DAKOTA ARRIVES.

Inventions from the early 40s

The 1940s is arguably one of the most important decades of the past century. War and the technology that would follow changed people's lives on a grand scale, creating everything from new industries to Countries. The events in the 1940s rippled across history, and without looking too hard, you can still feel the events of this decade.

Aerosol can

The concept of an aerosol goes way back to the 1790s, the first patent granted in 1927 however it wasn't until 1941 that the aerosol can was first put to effective use by Lyle Goodhue & William Sullivan who are widely credited as inventors of the modern spray can. It was created during WWII as a means to kill malaria carrying bugs for soldiers.

Velcro

Another great example of biomimicry, velcro had a profound impact on how we create clothing as well as some of our most standard daily items. Created by mountaineer and inventor George de Mestral, his inspiration came from the burrs that attached to his dog when he went out for a walk.

CBS & Peter Goldmark pioneered a system which transmitted an image in each of the 3 primary colours. Their TV was based on John Logie Bairds designs.

Mobile Phones

Surprised? While the first commercially viable phone did not come into existence until 1983. In 1947, T&T proposed that the FCC allocate a large number of radio-spectrum frequencies so that widespread mobile telephone service would become feasible. It was Bell Laboratories that had introduced the idea of cellular communications in 1947 with police car technology.

The Jeep

Was designed in 1940 in just 18 hrs by Karl Probst. Production of the first prototype took just 72 days.

The Z3 - May 12th 1941

Konrad Zuse The Z3 was the world's first working programmable, fully automatic digital computer. It was also the first computer-controlled by software. The computer itself was built with 2,600 relays implementing a 22-bit word length that operated at an impressive clock frequency of approximately 4-5 Hz.

Inventions from the early 40s

Atomic Bomb

"I am become Death, the destroyer of worlds." These were the words that theoretical physicist, J. Robert Oppenheimer, uttered after seeing the test of his atomic bomb. This line actually comes from a Hindu famous scripture, later to be proven to be a mistranslation. Nevertheless, the atomic bomb and its destructive power were unprecedented, changing the course of WWII, the coming Cold War, and the course of history.

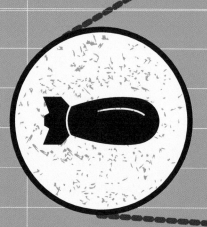

The Kidney Dialysis Machine

Willem Johan Pim Kolff accomplished a lot in his lifetime becoming both a pioneer in the field of hemodialysis and the interesting field of artificial organs. During the Second World War, he made major discoveries in the field of dialysis for kidney; the technology and research that would go on to save countless lives.

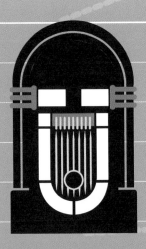

The juke box

Though the first coin-operated jukebox was already around in the 1890s, the jukebox you know today did not appear until the 1940s. The jukebox was so popular that at some point nearly ⅔ of all American-produced records were being played in jukeboxes across the country.

Microwave

Percy Spence is the man that brought the microwave over into existence in 1947. The invention was actually based off of radar technology that was created during the war. However, it was still far from the microwave that you love today. The countertop friendly microwave did not make its way to the market until 1967.

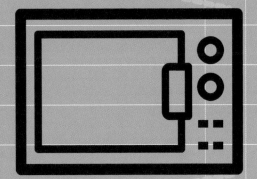

The V campaign

It was the symbol that united the British people during the darkest days of World War Two. Prime Minister Winston Churchill made the V for Victory hand gesture one of the defining images of defiance during the bloody conflict.

Today, the gesture is more commonly acknowledged as meaning 'peace' but back in 1941 it was much more powerful.

The famous wartime symbol is now synonymous with Churchill, although he wasn't the one who came up with it.

The powerful sign was first dreamt up in Belgium a year before it swept across Europe and into Britain. Winston Churchill first used the V for Victory sign on July 19, 1941.

However, while the sign should be made with the palm facing outwards, Churchill was often holding a cigar and could be seen making the gesture with his palm facing towards him. It was reported that as a member of the upper classes, initially Churchill was said to be unaware of its rude meaning.

But even after one of his staff told him that making the sign with his palm facing inwards meant 'up yours' - he still refused to stop using it that way. Churchill's private secretary, John Colville, wrote at the time in his private diaries: "The PM will give the V-sign with two fingers in spite

Winston Churchill

of representations repeatedly made to him that this gesture has quite another significance."

The double meaning - V for Victory or 'stick it up the Germans' became part of the national consciousness and stuck for the rest of the war.

Winston Churchill

Sir Winston Leonard Spencer Churchill (30 November 1874 – 24 January 1965) was a British statesman, army officer, and writer. He was Prime Minister of the United Kingdom from 1940 to 1945, when he led the country to victory in the Second World War, and again from 1951 to 1955 Of mixed English and American parentage, Churchill was born in Oxfordshire to a wealthy, aristocratic family. He joined the British Army in 1895 and saw action in British India, the Anglo-Sudan War, and the Second Boer War, gaining fame as a war correspondent and writing books about his campaigns.

Evacuation

During 1941 many British children were living with host families as evacuees. By the end of the war around 3.5 million had experienced evacuation.

There were 3 rounds of evacuation the first in 1939. However initially as there were no immediate bombings the children came home. During the blitz of autumn 1940 children were again sent away for safety.

Many pregnant women were also evacuated - there were many babies born in the countryside that soon returned to the cities when it was safe.

The Blitz

The heavy and frequent bombing attacks on London and other cities was known as the 'Blitz'. Night after night, from September 1940 until May 1941, German bombers attacked British cities, ports and industrial areas.

London was bombed ever day and night, bar one, for 11 weeks. One third of London was destroyed.

Blitz is a shorten form of the German word 'Blitzkrieg' (lightning war). Other cities and towns were also heavily bombed, including Swansea, Cardiff, Bristol, Southampton, Plymouth, Birmingham, Coventry and Liverpool. One devastating raid on Coventry in November 1940 was the biggest air-raid the world had ever seen. 4,330 homes were destroyed and 554 people killed. At one point during the night 200 separate fires burned in the city.

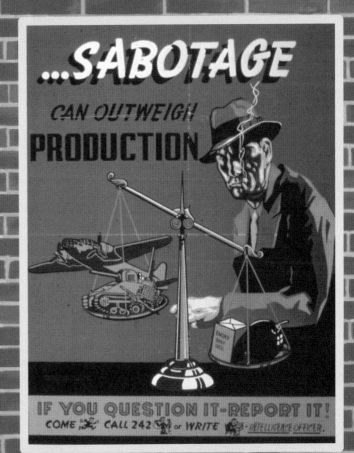

CITY OF LONDON POLICE
DANGER
UNEXPLODED BOMB

BETTER POT-LUCK with Churchill today

THAN HUMBLE PIE under Hitler tomorrow

DON'T WASTE FOOD!

PUBLIC SHELTERS IN VAULTS UNDER PAVEMENTS IN THIS STREET

'Beat FIREBOMB FRITZ'

BRITAIN SHALL NOT BURN

IS BRITAIN'S

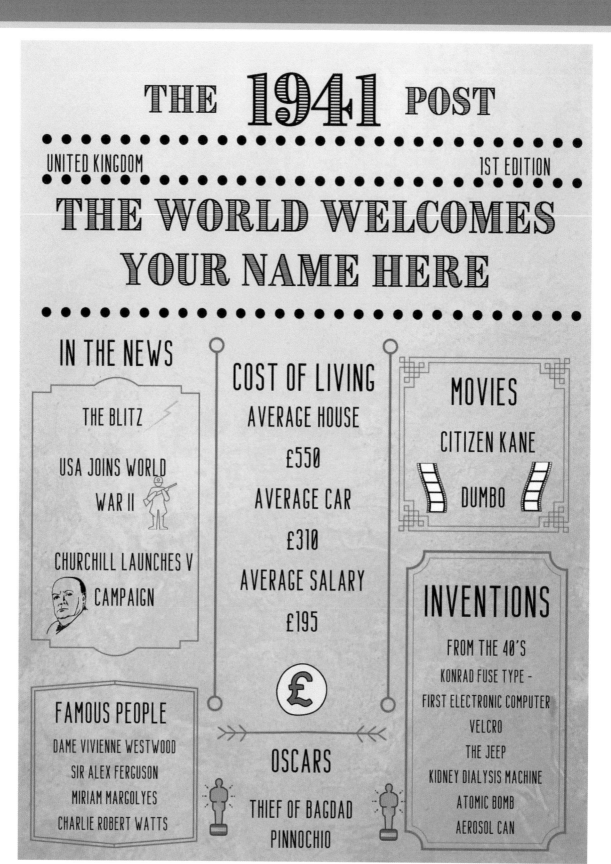

Little Pips Press

How to claim your free gift:

Visit the following address:

https://www.subscribepage.com/littlepipspress1941

Type in your email to receive your link to download the editable poster that you can print out at home or at a local printers. Whether your celebrating at home or elsewhere this will help make an occasion of your special day. This can even be framed as a memento of your special day.

The poster can be edited to include your name and can be printed any size.

Little Pips Press is a family run business. Our range of milestone books includes:

We hope you have a great Birthday!

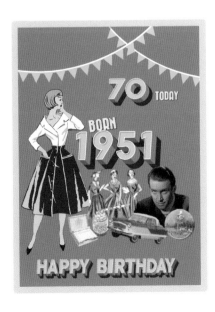

The legal stuff

Attribution for photo images goes to the following talented photographers under the creative commons licenses specified:

Printed in Great Britain
by Amazon